Training Your Diabetic Alert Dog
Rita Martinez and Susan M. Barns

Published by Rita Martinez and Susan M. Barns

Copyright 2013 Rita Martinez and Susan M. Barns

First Edition

Cover photo "Trey," cover design: Bill Manns
Interior photographs: Rita Martinez
Jacket design: Paul Chernoch

organization or website may provide or recommendations it may make. Further, readers should be aware that Internet websites listed in this work may have changed or disappeared between when this work was written and when it was read.

While we recognize that dogs of either gender can make excellent diabetic alert dogs, for the sake of brevity, we refer to dogs as "he/him" in this work.

eBook: ISBN-10: 098885080X   ISBN-13: 978-0-9888508-0-4
Print book: ISBN-10: 0988850818   ISBN-13: 978-0-9888508-1-1

To contact Rita Martinez, please visit her website:
http://www.clickincanines.com

Training Your Diabetic Alert Dog
Table of Contents

Chapter 9: Training games
- o   Training games
- o   Scent maintenance games

Chapter 10: Additional skills
- o   Third-party alerts/Go for Help
- o   Retrieve blood glucose meter, juice box, glucose tablets, etc.
- o   Finding/trailing the diabetic

Chapter 11: Troubleshooting
- o   Missed alerts
- o   False alerts
- o   Multiple alerts
- o   Alerts on strangers in public

Chapter 12: Conclusion

Appendix and Glossary
About the Authors/Acknowledgements

Chapter 1

Introduction

This book is lovingly written to help you train your diabetic alert dog (DAD). It is not meant to be an alternative to working with a professional trainer. The purpose here is to provide information and examples of a program to help you and your trainer reach your goals with your dog. We want to pass on as much information as possible so you can avoid trouble along the way.

If you are working with a new dog or considering acquiring one, you will find valuable information to guide you through the process. If you have a dog from an organization that is already trained, this book can aid in your upkeep work and exercises. If you are a trainer asked to help a handler with their dog, here is your guide for the basics. This is not, however, a trainers' manual. *Training Your Diabetic Alert Dog* is written for the diabetic dog handler.

This book is limited to the diabetic alert dog arena. We are not including instructions for the public access training that is so critical for the service dog. It is recommended that you work with a knowledgeable positive reinforcement trainer familiar with such training. All service dog teams must be absolutely credible in public.

Benefits of diabetic alert dogs

Maintaining tight control over blood glucose (BG) changes is the goal of the diabetic. The dog is an additional tool to that end. Electronic instruments such as meters and continuous glucose monitors (CGMs) are also wonderful aids. All the instruments in the world will not make the disease go away, but utilizing as many as possible is often what the individual wants.

Dogs are not machines. They aren't perfect — nor are their human handlers. They are, however, able to detect and alert to blood glucose events. DADs often alert to changes in blood glucose levels well before meters and monitors show low or high readings, allowing the handler to treat appropriately and avoid large BG spikes. Many report a much improved hemoglobin A1c (HbA1c) after the addition of a trained alert dog. When BG testing is difficult, such as at night or while driving, dogs can alert. Dogs can also be trained to provide alerts to "third parties" other than the handler, notifying family members or others that assistance is needed. And when a meter, monitor or pump fails (as all electronic devices can), a trained dog can provide life-saving information.

Living with a service dog

A service dog can be a wonderful asset for someone with a disability, but it is always good to go into anything with your eyes open from the beginning. Many factors come into play with the use of a service dog. These dogs can be life-saving partners, but they come with needs and can change every aspect of your life. Below are some things to think about.

Do you like dogs — enough to share your life with one 24/7? These dogs are not simply a tool; they are individual intelligent creatures with their own set of needs. They become a part of every portion of your everyday life. Are you ready for that kind of sharing?

A service dog is on call 24/7 for you. **Are you ready to be equally dedicated to your dog?** They aren't machines with an off switch, they are living partners. You will be responsible for all of your dog's needs at all times. That means there are frequently times that it will be inconvenient.

Having a service dog is like growing a new appendage. You are no longer just you — you are a *we*. You will have to consider where your dog can walk, sit or stand and be safely out of harm's way. You will have to seek appropriate places for your dog to relieve himself. You have to make sure the dog has a place to be comfortable with you, yet safe from heat or cold or tight quarters, etc. Yes, that means even in public restrooms...

You are responsible for all of your dog's needs, both on duty and off.

Are you ready and able to care for your dog's physical requirements? Dogs need proper exercise, grooming, bathing, feeding and off-duty outlets. There also needs to be a provision for the financial responsibility of regular healthcare and preventative medicine.

Are you aware that there are licenses, equipment, and miscellaneous **costs associated with having a working dog?**

Are there other animals in the home? Keep in mind that bringing in a working partner while there are other animals in the home will change the dynamics. Are the current animals likely to adapt easily? Does the rest of your family want an addition to the household?

Are you ready and able to participate in continued training to keep the skills from degrading? Training is never finished — maintenance is forever.

Are you prepared to do more BG testing everyday if necessary? Training your DAD will initially require that you monitor your diabetes more closely than you may be doing currently.

Are you aware of the public issues you will encounter? You will forever be answering the same questions and educating the general public about service dogs. Business owners may question your right to enter their establishments. Difficulties in using public transportation are common. People with allergies or fear of dogs will often object to the presence of your DAD. Your diabetes will no longer be "invisible," a service dog will draw attention to you no matter how well behaved he may be.

And lastly, **are you comfortable with the liability** of having your dog with you in all situations in public?

These questions are not meant to discourage you from having a service dog. But it is wise to approach something this important with real thought. Having a dog as a working partner is a commitment that lasts many years. It is a decision that needs careful consideration.

Training a DAD isn't for everyone...

Training your own diabetic alert dog is a sizable commitment. It is absolutely fine to admit that you may not be up for the task. Chances are you are not a dog trainer by profession and it is common for well-meaning family members to encourage to the point of pressure. Living with diabetes is difficult on its own, so to add the task of training an alert dog is simply not for everyone. If you fall into the category of uncertainty, please do not feel like you will disappoint others. Take on a mission like this only if you feel physically and mentally up to the challenge. It is like raising a child with whom you have no common language and requires patience and a good sense of humor to accomplish success. Young mothers with diabetic children usually find that the commitment required in having a DAD plus the daily care of the child or children is shocking. Wanting and needing a DAD is one thing — making it happen is quite another.

Sources of professionally trained DADs

Organizations are an alternative source for those who cannot do this themselves. There are a growing number of trainers and programs responding to the diabetic community's interest in alert dogs. While some have approached this professionally and are producing credible working DADs, sadly, others are taking advantage of the public's desire for a "quick fix" and lack of information by selling (often for very high prices) unskilled dogs with minimal (or no) training. Professional service dog programs typically take 1.5 to 2 years to train a finished working DAD, and work with the client through a 2-week team training program (and beyond).

We urge you to do "due diligence" on any program in which you are interested! Some guidelines on finding a reputable program can be found in the Appendix. Accredited programs that provide trained DADs are listed on The Assistance Dogs International (ADI) website (see Appendix). Do your research; training your own dog is not the only option available.

Finding a trainer

The internet is a wonderful place to search for a trainer or a training facility. However, just because there is an online presence with a nice looking website does not guarantee quality training. Do your due diligence just as you would if you were buying a car or a home. Inquire about training credentials and check the responses. Ask for references and check them well. A good resource for finding accredited trainers is the Certification Council for Professional Dog Trainers (see Appendix). Local service dog agencies may also be able to refer you to a private trainer, or may provide classes for owner-trainers. The ADI website lists accredited service dog agencies in the US and internationally (see Appendix).

Selecting a trainer

What are you looking for? You want a trainer who you feel comfortable with and that dogs seem comfortable with as well. Observe a class and watch how the dogs and students work with the trainer. Are they all enjoying the exercises? Is the trainer able to teach students how to train without force or punishment? Has the trainer done any scent work with dogs? Is the trainer comfortable with your questions? Will they be accessible to you in between lessons if you have questions or issues?

Check for service dog experience, particularly with regard to public access work. This is a very specialized field of training, and few trainers understand the nature and extent of training necessary, unless they have trained service dogs previously.

Training philosophy is very important for a potential service dog who will be expected to work 24/7 and alert without being cued to do so. Look for a trainer who is committed to positive reinforcement training. It is neither necessary nor desirable to use force, pain or intimidation to train dogs. Indeed, use of aversive methods can slow the learning process considerably, and produce a dog who is afraid to "disobey" when necessary to attend to your needs. A dog who is afraid to get up from a Down/Stay in order to alert you to changes in your BG is of limited use as a DAD. Finding a trainer who can coach you in positive ways to motivate your dog to work with enthusiasm and joy is critical to training reliable diabetic alert work.

Your part in the training process

Finding a good trainer is just the beginning of the journey, and your success in training a DAD will be due, in large part, to the effort and time you put into the training. **Be prepared to devote several hours a week for a year or more to training your dog, both at home and in public.** When working with a trainer, be sure you can communicate well with him or her, ask questions whenever necessary, and be sure you understand the exercises you are given to practice before your lesson is over.

Finally, be sure to educate your trainer about your diabetes, as most will be unfamiliar with the disease and its effects. Don't be shy about this! Let them know your needs and desires, and help them to understand how fluctuations in your BG change your health and mental status. Diabetes affects how and when you will train, can interfere with learning and following through with instructions, and of course, impacts what you will be training your dog to do. Be sure to find a trainer who is open to learning about diabetes as a critical part of helping you train your DAD.

>>>>>>>><<<<<<<<

Chapter 2

Selecting a dog for diabetic alert training

The importance of selecting a suitable dog for diabetic alert service work cannot be overemphasized. Your DAD must not only be willing and able to respond to your BG changes 24/7, but must also be comfortable, focused, well-behaved and trained to accompany you in all your daily activities, at home and in public. This is asking a lot of any dog, and **it is unfair and irresponsible to require a dog with an unsuitable temperament to work in situations in which he is uncomfortable.**

In our experience, very few dogs are truly suited for service work. For reference, long-standing guide and assistance dog programs with decades of experience breeding, raising and training dogs for service work typically wash out over 75% of the dogs they breed! Programs that utilize shelter dogs assess dozens of dogs before selecting one for training, and most of those chosen are released before completing service dog training. *The time and effort you put in up-front in selecting your dog is the single most important thing you can do to ensure your success in training a DAD.*

This section will outline what we feel are the most important considerations in selecting a dog for DAD training. This is a complex topic, and we cannot offer definitive guidance. Additional resources are listed in the Appendix, and it is well worth your time to research the topic thoroughly.

Age and gender
Our preference is to start DAD training as early as possible. Puppies of 10 weeks of age can be started on scent work, and the sooner that pups get going making positive associations with scent, the better. Working with a puppy also allows you to start "from scratch" in socializing your pup to the world he will work in, and in training appropriate service dog behaviors.

The pitfall of starting with puppies is that it is somewhat difficult to predict adult temperament and health at a young age. Despite careful selection and training, sometimes even very promising pups develop behavior and/or health issues in adolescence and adulthood that make them unsuitable for service work. If obtaining a puppy, stack the deck in your favor by selecting one from a responsible breeder who focuses on health, temperament and early socialization in breeding and raising pups.

What about older pups/dogs? A few considerations come into play here. The first is that training your DAD will take at least a year of hard effort, including training for public access work. Starting with an older dog means potentially retiring your DAD after only a few years of service, and starting over with another dog. In addition, adult dogs may have learned undesirable behaviors (such as barking at other dogs, pulling on leash, etc.) that will have to be retrained in order to be successful service dogs. Perhaps most importantly, starting with an older dog means missing the critical period of socialization for puppies, during which the pup can be exposed to and learn to accept all the environments he will encounter as an adult working dog.

On the other hand, older pups/dogs are more of a "known quantity" with respect to temperament, behavior and health. A well-socialized, healthy adult dog without behavior issues may make an excellent candidate for DAD training.

The best gender for a DAD is...both! We have had equal success in training male and female dogs for service work. This is the least critical factor in selecting a dog for training. Individual temperament far outweighs any gender differences.

Breed

Many different breeds of dogs have been successfully trained for DAD work. Again, individual temperament differences are more critical overall than are breed tendencies. In general, dogs from the working breeds (retrievers, terriers, herding breeds), which have been selected for hundreds of years for their ability to work with/for humans, are most likely to succeed. Within each breed, however, there can be a huge range of temperaments. Dogs bred for extreme working or sport activities (such as field trials, protection sports or agility) often have too much energy to be happy as service dogs. In contrast, dogs bred to be working companions (gun dogs, stock herding dogs, etc.) can be better choices.

Dogs from working, herding and sporting breeds are among those suitable for DAD work.

Mixed-breed dogs are also capable of becoming DADs. Choosing a dog that is a mix of the above breed types is a reasonable way to go, although it is not always easy to determine a dog's breed heritage. If you decide to adopt a shelter dog for training as a DAD, be aware that it is very difficult to adequately assess a dog's true temperament in the shelter environment. Many dogs behave very differently in the shelter, and for several weeks or months after adoption, than they do after settling in to a home environment. It may take many months to find a dog with the right temperament for service work, and even after careful selection, you may find that the dog is unsuited to the work. Of course, this is also true of pure-bred dogs.

We caution against selecting dogs from breeds with broad, short noses (brachycephalic), such as Pugs, Bulldogs, and Pekingese. In addition to having smaller noses, with potentially fewer scent receptors, these breeds often have difficulty with breathing and thermoregulation (staying cool), making working life difficult.

Short-nosed, or brachycephalic, breeds may have a reduced ability to scent.

Beyond scenting ability, **other factors may influence your breed choice.** Smaller dogs can be easier to maintain and transport than very large dogs. Giant breeds tend to have shorter working lives, and may lack the stamina to keep up with an active handler. Small dogs can find working in public very scary, and handlers with small, non-traditional service dogs may be questioned in public more often. Overall, however, it is most important for you to select a dog that you can live and work with comfortably, and whose mental and physical needs you can easily meet.

Desired traits for DAD work

There are a few characteristics that may help a dog succeed in diabetic alert work:

- **A tendency to use his nose** to explore the world. A dog who tends to be "sniffy," checking out things in a new place by smelling them and being drawn towards interesting odors, may be more likely to detect and respond to changes in BG scents. He need not be obsessed or overstimulated by smells, but it is helpful if he "sees the world through his nose," rather than being attracted to sights or sounds.

- Similarly, a dog who **stays close to you** during the day, following from room to room or staying in visual range, has a better chance of detecting your lows and highs than one who chooses to stay outside all day. When out in public, a dog that can remain focused on you is also likely to be more able to detect and alert.

- Since alert work is 24/7, a DAD needs **sufficient energy and enthusiasm** to work all day, although of course, you will need to provide adequate opportunities for relaxation and sleep. Ideally, the dog should not sleep so soundly that he cannot awaken to alert during the night.

- In order to effectively alert you when you are mentally impaired, a certain amount of **tenacity** can be very beneficial. This can be trained to a certain extent, but it can be easier if it is inherent in the dog. A dog that continues to show interest in a task after two repetitions is desirable.

Desired traits for service dog work

The standards for acceptable behavior of service dogs working in public settings are very high, and will likely require more of your training time and effort than teaching DAD skills. For reference, we suggest that you review the Assistance Dogs International (ADI) "Minimum Standards for Assistance Dogs in Public" (see Appendix). Your service dog must be calm, quiet, unobtrusive and able to focus and work comfortably in all public settings. This can require a great deal of confidence and self-control from even the most well-trained dog, and starting out with a dog having these qualities can make your training job much easier, and your dog's working life much more enjoyable.

A short list of desired qualities for a diabetic alert service dog includes:

- **Social and Tolerant** — Behaves in a friendly manner towards all people and dogs, both familiar and unfamiliar. No aggression or fear should be displayed. Permits petting by strangers, remaining friendly and polite during greeting.

- **Confident** — Relaxed and certain in all normal situations and environments. Does not exhibit overly fearful behavior towards any common stimuli, including sights and sounds. Should not cower, flee, bark, spook, avoid or overreact to any things or events in the environment including noises, objects, animals, vehicles, surfaces, machines, etc.

- **Focused** — Able to concentrate on, and take direction from, the handler in all environments. Not overly distracted by other people, dogs, animals, traffic, etc.

- **Polite** — Fully housetrained in all environments, and trained to eliminate on command.

   Resilient — Recovers quickly in all situations and environments. Must not be reactive or fall apart from the many surprise events that occur in public work.

- **Olfactory** — Has a sincere interest in the world through the nose.

In general, a service dog needs to be stable in temperament, easygoing and confident in all settings. Your DAD may encounter novel and unpredictable situations every day, and must meet them all with equanimity. This is important not only for your sake, so that the dog can remain focused on detecting and alerting to your BG changes, but also for the dog's mental and emotional well-being. Regardless of training, a dog that is chronically nervous or stressed in his working environment will break down emotionally and physically over time. In addition, a dog who feels unsafe is more likely to act out in unacceptable ways such as barking, growling, bolting and lunging. Behavior seen as threatening or disruptive can be grounds for denial of access rights with your dog, and can contribute to service dogs being scrutinized and questioned.

Service dogs must accompany their owners into many busy places, yet remain calm and focused.

It is recommended that you train your dog to a sufficient level to pass ADI's "Public Access Test" (see Appendix). This test is considered the industry standard for service dog behavior and training, and helps insure that your dog has the temperament and skills to behave appropriately in public.

Assessing dog behavior

We highly recommend enlisting the help of a service dog organization or trainer, or an experienced trainer or behaviorist who is familiar with service dog work and behavior assessment, in evaluating a puppy or dog. Resources are listed in the Appendix. Be prepared to spend several months searching for and assessing many dogs in order to select one of appropriate temperament. It will be time well spent.

If you already have a dog you are considering for DAD training, observing your dog with the guidelines outlined above is a good start to assessing his suitability for service work. It is, however, difficult to stand outside the box and be unbiased yet very easy to see just what you want to see. We recommend having the dog evaluated by a professional, and one who is familiar with Suzanne Clothier's Animal Response Assessment Tool (CARAT) method would be ideal. Evaluating for a working dog is different from the older-style puppy temperament tests. You can't test temperament, but characteristics can be looked at and evaluated.

Please note also that it is important that your dog be fundamentally healthy before considering training him for service work. Many health conditions can greatly alter behavior in dogs. Be sure to have your veterinarian check your dog for issues (diseases, orthopedic conditions, etc.) that might impact his working ability or temperament.

"Red flags"

In selecting a puppy or dog for DAD work in public, there are some behavior issues to look for and avoid. The most difficult issue to work with is fear, which may appear as shyness, aggression or "shutting down" ("flight, fight or freeze"). If the dog shows signs of wanting to flee, is slow to warm up to people or barks repeatedly/acts aggressively towards other dogs, people, animals, sounds, objects, etc. it will be difficult to train him to be comfortable in public settings. Of course, it is natural for puppies and new dogs to show some caution towards novel things, environments, dogs and people, but it should not be extreme, and the dog should relax and adjust quickly. Assessing the level of fear in dogs can be difficult, and again, we suggest getting the advice of an experienced trainer or behaviorist who can observe your dog's behavior directly. The Canine Behavioral Assessment and Research Questionnaire (C-BARQ; see Appendix) also provides some assessment of fearful tendencies.

Although easier to work with than fear, dogs with a great deal of energy, or who are overly friendly towards other dogs and people also pose some training challenges. Similarly, dogs who are highly distracted by motion (bicycles, joggers, vehicles), other animals (birds, squirrels, cats, dogs), or anything else in the environment may have trouble focusing on your BG or taking cues from you.

Chapter 3

Scent and canine scenting

The dog's sense of smell is astounding, both in its ability to detect odors too faint for us to notice, and its ability to identify and distinguish smells. It is thought that the dog's sensitivity to odors may be hundreds or thousands of times better than our own. This incredible scenting ability allows dogs to find minute amounts of narcotics, sniff out hidden bombs and buried landmines, and locate survivors in the rubble of collapsed buildings. Your dog has this ability, too, and can be trained to detect your BG changes. Understanding this ability, as well as learning about the nature of scent, will help you to train your dog.

How dogs scent

Sense of smell is a dog's primary sense. Much like humans use vision, a dog takes in most of his information about the world through his nose. Whereas humans have about 5 million scent receptors in our noses, dogs have as many as 220 million receptors! The percentage of a dog's brain devoted to processing smells is thought to be 40 times larger than that of humans. Dogs even have a special organ, called the vomeronasal organ, in the roof of their mouths that allow them to detect smells through the mouth.

The dog's nose is normally cool and moist, and mucus inside the nose helps to trap scent and transport it to special nerve cells called receptors. The area covered by the receptors is large, extending from the end of the nose all the way back to the eyes, and wraps around many folded bony layers called turbinates. When a dog encounters a scent he begins rapid sniffing, which increases the amount of air, and therefore scent, that enters the nose. The shape of the nose interior, together with the moist mucus, helps to trap and concentrate scent. Interaction of the scent molecules with receptor cells sends information to the brain for processing and storage.

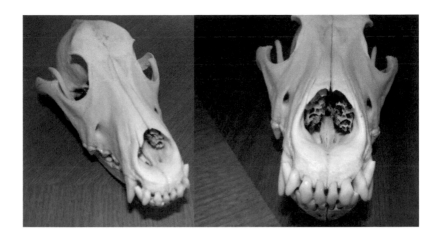

Bony folds in the dog's nose, called turbinates, provide a large surface area for scent receptors.

Dogs can readily learn to identify an odor from a single exposure to it, and can remember smells for years thereafter. They can even detect odors separately with their right and left nostrils, and use the information to determine the direction from which an odor is coming.

What is "diabetic scent?"

At this time, scientists do not know exactly what odors dogs detect when they sense changes in BG. Based on dogs' behavior and our ability to train them, it appears that rapid falls or rises in BG cause the body to produce different chemicals that appear in breath, saliva and sweat (and probably other places as well). The chemicals probably differ depending on whether a person's BG is changing slowly or rapidly, and whether they are going low or high. This allows dogs to detect rapid changes that are potentially dangerous, and they can be trained to signal the direction of the change (low or high). Dogs can sense these changes not only in Type I diabetics, but also in Type II diabetics and people with blood sugar changes unrelated to diabetes. It is also possible that dogs can detect and alert to non-odor related signals from the diabetic, such as changes in behavior, motion or breathing.

Scent in the environment

It is helpful to know some basics about how scent behaves in the environment in order to effectively train your DAD. The chemicals that make up scent must leave your body (or a scent sample), travel through the air and be detected by the dog. Although we cannot see it, it can be useful to think of scent moving like smoke or fog.

Scent moves like smoke in the environment, depending on air currents.

Scent moves with air currents and wind, so it is helpful to keep in mind which way the air is moving when training. Indoor environments are very tricky with regard to air currents. Forced air heat or cooling, windows with or without sun, doorways, furniture and human motion all influence air currents. And keep in mind that the air may be moving differently down at your dog's level. In short, this means that you cannot effectively guess just where the scent has dispersed.

At all times, remember that you cannot see or smell the scent yourself. **You can never be sure that your dog should be noticing the scent, only the dog knows!** You will have to watch and understand your dog's response and develop some trust. We will discuss this critical skill in more detail later in this book.

DAD alerts vs. BG meters and continuous glucose monitors

It is very important to understand how alerts from your DAD will differ from the information provided by your BG meter and/or CGM. Since dogs can detect when your BG is dropping or rising, they will often alert when your meter or monitor reads in the "normal" range. This can be confusing at first, but is actually a great help, as it allows you to treat yourself before you go dangerously low or high. There is a permitted margin of error (up to 20%) with meters. Alert dogs and technical instruments are all part of the information available to you. A well-trained dog is a wonderful tool and doesn't require batteries, test strips or special sensors, but is not to be considered the only tool in your toolbox.

Factors affecting DAD work

In addition to the factors that affect scent movement, described above, there are many things that can alter your dog's ability to alert to your BG changes. As noted, a dog's nose must be moist to work well. Conditions which dry the nose, such as dehydration, will reduce the dog's ability to smell, so it is important to be sure your dog has enough water at all times. Other conditions which afflict the nose, such as infection, cancer, foreign bodies, and age will also reduce the ability to smell. Dogs cannot smell as well when they are panting as when they are breathing normally, so it is good to keep your dog cool (for many reasons).

Beyond physical issues that affect scenting ability, there are other considerations that impact a dog's alerting. More generally, any condition which affects your dog's health may impair his ability to alert you. During times of illness, you should plan to monitor and manage your diabetes more closely, as your dog may be less able to help. If your dog is overly distracted by or anxious about his environment, he may not notice your BG changes, or be able to alert to them. Your dog's level of fatigue will also influence his ability to alert. This is especially important in nighttime alerts. If your dog is exhausted and sleeps very soundly, it can be more difficult for him to waken to alert. If you have a very active life, it may be a good idea to give your dog rest/nap breaks during the day, during which he can get uninterrupted sleep (you will need to manage your diabetes yourself during these periods). No one can truly work 24/7!

Diabetic alert work vs. other canine detection jobs

Although there is some overlap, training your dog to alert to changes in BG is quite different from more "traditional" canine detection work, such as drug or bomb sniffing. For one thing, there is usually an abundance of scent for the DAD to perceive; he does not need to hunt for minute quantities of odor. In addition, the dog does not need to search in order to find the source of the scent, it is easy to find (it's you!). This is an important distinction to note: in training DADs we are creating "tattle tale" dogs, with an emphasis on training a strong alert, not training search dogs. The BG scent itself is really just a cue that tells your dog to perform the alert behavior — a readily available cue that he does not need to search for.

Chapter 4

Scent sample collection, storage and use

Training your dog to detect and alert to changes in your blood glucose levels is greatly simplified by using scent samples. If you have collected scent samples when your BG is low and high, and stored them for training use, you can train when it is convenient to do so, when you are thinking clearly and can carry out well-planned training sessions. We encourage you to collect and store many samples so that you will be able to train whenever you need to. Sample collection, storage and use is fairly simple, but it is important to take some care with the process.

What to sample

It is possible to train your dog using several different sources of scent, including saliva, sweat and breath. We recommend the use of **saliva** as it is easily obtained, stored and used, and turns over rapidly in the body, responding quickly to changes in BG levels. We discourage the use of blood test strips as blood tends to degrade very rapidly.

When to sample

You may collect samples whenever your BG is low or high. In general, this means at BG levels below 75 and above 200. You should attempt to collect the samples when your BG is either dropping (for low BG samples) or rising (for high BG samples). It is important to collect the samples BEFORE you have treated your low or high with food (glucose) or insulin.

Sampling equipment

There are many ways to collect samples, and you may wish to modify our suggestions depending on the equipment you have available. We recommend using the following items:

- Clean, unscented **cotton pads** (rounds or squares) or cotton balls. Non-sterile is fine.

- Clean, tightly sealing **plastic tubes**. BG test strip vials work well for this. You may reuse tubes after washing with detergent in tap water, rinsing well and drying. Reuse low BG tubes for low samples, and high BG tubes for high samples. Mark the tubes clearly. Tubes may also be set in the sun to dry and air for a few hours to dilute residual scent.

- Clean, tightly-sealing **containers to hold the tubes**, one for low, one for high. Glass mason jars and clean plastic food storage containers (Tupperware™) work well. Ideally the container should not be much larger than the tubes. Use the same care as used with the tubes.

- A **way to mark the tubes** and containers, such as indelible markers ("Sharpies™") and/or tape and ink pen. Label all pieces so that it is clear which pieces go together.

- A **freezer** to store the samples. A non-frost-free freezer is ideal, but any freezer will work.

Suggested equipment for sampling includes [clockwise from top] clean cotton pads, indelible marker, outer container [jar] with lid and test strip tube

Sampling and storage

After you have tested your blood and determined that your BG is low or high, follow these guidelines for sampling:

- **Wash your hands well**, preferably with unscented soap.

- **Moisten a pad with saliva**. You may take multiple samples at once. If you find little saliva available, as happens with many high events, you can swab the pad around the inside of the mouth.

- **Place the pad in a tube** and seal the tube.

- **Mark the tube** with the BG number and the date of collection.

- **Place the tube in a glass or plastic container**, using a separate marked container for low and high BG. You may store low samples together, and high samples together if necessary, but keeping the individual tubes in separate containers is preferred.

- **Store containers in freezer** for up to 6 months.

Using samples

- **When you are ready to train**, remove the container with the sample tube (or an individual sample tube from container of multiple tubes) from the freezer and allow it to thaw for a few minutes, keeping the tube closed. Follow the directions in the "Training" section of this guide for using the samples.

- **When you are done with training**, you may store the sample in a refrigerator if you will be training again later the same day. When you are done training for the day, mark the tube you have used (to indicate that you have thawed it once) and place it back in the freezer container.

As a general guideline, we recommend thawing and refreezing a sample no more than three times before discarding it. However, if you have any reason to think that the sample is no longer good, due to drying out, becoming contaminated, molding, or if your dog stops responding as you think he should to the sample, discard it.

Take good care of your samples!

When using the sample, take some care not to allow it to dry out, or become contaminated. For instance, if you are using treats to reward your dog, be careful not to dirty the sample tube by touching it after handling the treats. If you have stored it in your refrigerator, check to be sure the sample has not grown mold. If you have trained with a low BG sample, wash your hands or take other precautions before handling high BG samples. You need not be extreme in avoiding contamination, some will occur regardless, but being mindful in handling the samples will help your dog learn more quickly what scent it is he should pay attention to. Contamination with other scents presents the dog with a recipe (multiple scents) rather than an ingredient (target scent) to identify.

Chapter 5

Training: Basics and outline

Training a DAD is a labor-intensive process. The goal is to develop a working partner who will reliably alert you to BG fluctuations in all situations. A DAD is on duty 24/7 and must spontaneously respond to something that is invisible to the human. Alert dogs work differently from assistance dogs, as they have to think independently to warn of a BG event. Building the motivation for a dog to be unfailing for the long term comes only through good communication and the development of an understanding and trusting relationship.

A task of this magnitude is not likely accomplished through punishment-based training. Training with punishment tends to produce a dog who is reluctant to think on his own and offer behaviors without being told what to do. An alert dog is a true partner who volunteers vital information to keep you safe from wide BG swings. He must feel that he can do so safely, without fear of punishment or correction.

We have learned that a positive reinforcement-based approach is critical to the process of training an alert dog. A dog cannot be overpowered or punished into a motivated state. Dogs trained for other types of scent work, such as drug- and bomb-sniffing dogs, are also trained using positive reinforcement, as it is the preferred way to train the most reliable detection dogs.

Positive reinforcement (R+) training

If you have previously trained a dog with the use of choke collars, pinch collars or corrections, this will seem either foreign or a wonderful new method. The fact is, positive reinforcement training is not all that new, it has been used by animal trainers throughout history. It has gained popularity in dog training in recent years, and R+ trainers are now widespread. (We have listed resources in the Appendix [for Chapter 1] to assist you in finding a R+ trainer in your area.)

Reward-based training simply sets up and waits for the dog to do something right and reinforces it. This is a nice way to explain something to an animal who doesn't have a common language with us. Dogs learn through observation and trial and error. There is no value in adding force to the learning process – that only proves that you are poor at explaining what you want.

Rewards can be anything the dog thinks is worth working for. Food is often used to train new behaviors as it is quick and very motivating. Toys and games are effective but can also be disruptive in nature so are better suited for the end of a training session. Think of the reward as a paycheck. Few of us would continue to work if there was no longer a paycheck for us.

It is important to find out what your dog finds rewarding. Since DAD work can be life-saving, we want to use the most motivating rewards in training. Many people think their dog should be willing to work for praise or petting or a dog biscuit, but what the dog really wants is cheese! Or liver, or a toy, or a nice game of tug…you get the idea. Take a little time now to identify five things your dog thinks are worth working for, then rank them with #1 being the favorite. You will be using the top-ranked rewards for most of your DAD training.

Clicker training

Many think this is a new method of training. Actually, clicker training began during the 1940's with Keller and Marian Breland. Their company, Animal Behavior Enterprises, succeeded in training some 140 different species to perform various tasks using this approach. Karen Pryor has popularized the method over the past 20 years and these days there are many wonderful resources available to help you learn this powerful training method.

In simple terms, **the click is a marker.** Produced by a small, hand-held "clicker," the click marks what the dog did right and is followed by reinforcement. It is a clear, unemotional way to tell the dog "That's it!" so that he understands what it is we want. One click followed by reinforcement and then the opportunity to repeat the pattern is a clear way to train the dog. Without that information, the dog simply has to keep guessing about what you want and may become confused, frustrated or bored.

There are people who find the clicker cumbersome or who have reduced hand ability hindering its use. **A verbal marker can be used** instead. It is just not always timed as accurately and is inclined to express emotion. We have people that use a mouth click which is actually sort of a "cluck." Others use a word, such as "yes" or "good." The important thing to remember is to be consistent and always use the same word as the marker.

No matter what the tool, **timing is most important in marking a behavior.** The dog will learn that what he was doing at the instant of the marker is what he should repeat. This means you must be skilled at watching the dog so you deliver the marker in the most timely way. The delivery of the reinforcement does not have to be as quick. It's the marker that delivers the much-needed information to the dog.

Clicker- or marker-based training is integral to our process of training a DAD (and is also very helpful in training your dog to do other service dog skills). It is a mechanical skill that most people find fairly easy to learn. However, it is beyond the scope of this book to teach you how to clicker train. It is hoped that your trainer will be familiar in this approach, and can coach you in its use. We have provided excellent references in the Appendix for learning this skill, and we urge you to take a few days (or weeks) to become familiar with this method before starting to train your DAD. *Time taken now on this fundamental skill will pay off going forward, we guarantee!*

When to begin training
Training can and should begin as soon as you get your dog. If you have gotten a pup, he is probably nine or more weeks old when you bring him home and training can begin right away. Although we think of a puppy as a baby, he is mentally capable of learning quite effectively. Naturally you will not have stringent expectations, but you do not want to waste an important time in the pup's brain development by waiting.

If you have or acquire an older dog, there is also no need to wait. Establishing a training course to help you communicate and learn together is very beneficial to a new dog. They are a curious species and giving them something to do or learn is a wonderful way to establish boundaries and help them become comfortable.

General guidelines

Realistically, training is going on throughout the day as the dog or pup is learning about the new home environment and where the appropriate place for eliminating is, etc. Formal training sessions can be slipped in throughout the day as well. As you will be working tirelessly also on public access manners, you will be very busy for a year. Scent training is handled separately from the obedience work.

- **Planning** — Always have a plan for the session and stay focused on your goal. Decide what piece of the behavior you are going to work on and stay with that. Be sure that there is a good chance that your dog will do the behavior, don't make it too hard or too different from what he did last session.

    If the dog does something outside of your plan, do not be swayed away. Finish your session and then you can deal with the other issue in a separate training time. An example of this in obedience work would be working on a Stay. The dog is in a Sit and you give a Stay cue, but after a lengthy time he lays down but doesn't move the rear. If you were working on a Stay, the dog succeeded. Stay was the last cue given and that was the focus of your session. Position was not your goal. The dog did not self-release, but was not up to such an extended stay — which you could concentrate on in a different session.

- **Sessions** — A session is a series of repetitions. We advise you to stop if you have gotten three good responses. You may come back and do two or three more later in the day, but do not assume more is better. Scent lingers in the dog's nose for a time which makes working for ten reps of the scent quite redundant. Quit before the dog wants to stop — we want him happy about the next session.

- **Training frequency — One or two short sessions a day at least five days a week will give you results.** Working the pup on the scent is often very exciting for the handler, and it is tempting to work many repetitions in a session. This is absolutely not necessary for success and actually becomes a bit cumbersome to the dog who finds scent so basic. Do try to train most days of the week, but keep your sessions short, successful and fun.

- **"Only perfect practice makes perfect"** — Repetitions establish a pattern. Therefore, it is important to set the dog up for successful repetitions. Patterns are easily learned after three like repetitions. This is both good and bad. If the exercise was not set up well and the dog did poorly three times, then an undesired pattern was being established. *If your dog makes two errors in a row, stop training and change something in your training plan.*

- **Train, don't test** — This will be covered in more detail in the training section, but be aware at all times that you are "training" the dog, not "testing". We humans move to testing with vigor before allowing confidence in the skills — one of our human flaws.

- **Motivation** — Scent exercises should always be fun. Having an air of tension or seriousness can be perceived badly and misunderstood by the dog. Make sure the training is one of the highlights of the day. Motivation is built with fun and success and is something we need in an alert dog.

- **Be happy and enjoy the training** — This is a wonderful time for you and your dog to learn to communicate and enjoy the journey on a new path. Dogs love adventure, and you should make sure that you do as well. There will be times when you have to laugh at yourself and if you watch closely, you will probably see the dog do the same.

- **Have patience** — Don't train if you are upset or feeling off — it won't be as effective overall. Think about what you want to do and picture success in your mind rather than looking for failure. Remember, the dog is trying to figure out what is expected and so will make mistakes. We, too, make mistakes when learning something new.

- **Don't compare your dog with another dog** — They are as individual as we are. No two learn at exactly the same rate and each will have a spot that is more difficult than another. The important thing to remember is they all get to the end goal in pretty much the same time frame. None of our working dogs have been at all the same, yet they have all been successful at their jobs.

Training progression

Successful training advances in small steps. We must be sure that the foundation bricks are set before we add another layer on top. Knowing that the foundation is solid requires paying attention while being realistic and not seeing only what you wish. Moving ahead at a steady pace is the goal.

In outline, here is the training progression:

I.   Training will begin by establishing the **alert** behavior on verbal cue. This is the most critical of all the behaviors, as having a dog that does not have a definitive and reliable way to tell you there is an issue is akin to not having an alert dog at all.

II.   You will also train **two signals** to be reliable on verbal cue. These will be used to identify low and high BG situations.

III.   After the alert behavior is reliably on verbal cue, the **low BG scent will be imprinted**. This will begin the actual scent work.

IV.   After a few, short sessions imprinting the low scent, you will **train the dog to give the alert behavior in response to the scent.** This is a critical step, the basis for all DAD work going forward.

V.   As the alert chain becomes reliable, the **low signal will be added**. This signal will be given after the alert to indicate that your BG is low or dropping.

VI.   As this low chain is becoming comfortable, you will **imprint the high scent, and train the high alert/signal chain.** Since the chain will be the same as for the low except for the signal, this will be fast and easy by comparison.

VII.   This is the point where much **generalizing** will be necessary, so that the dog will be confident in alerting under any circumstances in any environment. Generalizing is the longer portion of the training, just as it is with obedience work.

We will go over night-time alerts, third-party alerts, and car alerts in a section following the "Training step by step" chapter.

>>>>>>><<<<<<<

Chapter 6

Training step by step

First, some basics

Progress in training — Something that is typically difficult to determine in the actual training is knowing when to move forward with the next step. There is a wonderful guide called the **"80%+ Rule."** Simply put, that means your dog must be succeeding 80% of the time before you increase difficulty or move to the next step. The easiest way to steadily move forward is to follow this method — you must have 80% success (four out of five, or eight out of ten repetitions) for three sessions <u>in a row</u> before proceeding. This routine will allow you to succeed without having to go back and rework older lessons that were not as solid as you thought. Moving faster will slow you in reaching your goal of a reliable DAD.

When to add the cue — How and when to add a verbal cue is so simple that many find it difficult. Since the dog does not have verbal language with us, we do not add the cue (verbal word) to the behavior until the behavior is happening regularly. Asking for something verbally before the dog is performing the behavior pattern is pointless.

When the behavior pattern is reliable, the word is paired while the behavior is happening, so the dog can "merge the verbal cue with the action." So, you will be telling the dog what they are doing, to aid them making that connection, prior to telling them what to do.

Trained over several sessions, it looks like this:

BEHAVIOR → CLICK → TREAT

BEHAVIOR + CUE → CLICK → TREAT

CUE → BEHAVIOR → CLICK → TREAT

Throughout the remainder of the book, C/T refers to Click followed by Treat.

I. Training the alert and signals

These three behaviors (one for alert, one each for low and high BG signals) are taught as tricks and are reliably on verbal cue before any scent work is begun.

The Alert

We cannot stress enough how important it is to have a rock solid alert behavior. Without that, there will be doubt and you will not have an effective alert that you or others will easily recognize. Guessing as to whether or not the dog gave an alert or was just trying to prompt you to play is not the sign of a well-trained DAD.

The purpose of the **alert** is for the dog to get your attention when he detects that your BG is out of range. Choosing an appropriate alert behavior takes some thought. The behaviors must work for you and the dog and must be discernible by you and also by others that may be summoned by the dog should you not be responsive. It should be effective at getting your attention even when you are distracted, asleep, busy or mentally foggy due to low or high BG. The behavior must not be disruptive in public or in a work environment. For this reason, the alert is never a bark.

- We do not generally advise a **bringsel** alert. A bringsel is cloth strip or tube that is attached to the dog's collar or to the diabetic person or left in a particular place in the home. It is retrieved by the dog and presented as an alert. Many dogs are not enthusiastic about this alert, and it requires the training of a special retrieve. Additional downsides of such an alert are the necessity of having a piece of equipment always available plus the need for an additional alert for night time and car use, when it is difficult to notice something in the dog's mouth.

- Many dogs love to use a **paw** to play or get your attention, and in some cases this can be an appropriate alert. But it has serious disadvantages as well. The paw alert is often mistaken as it tends to occur in other situations, and it can be overly zealous and scratch you or damage your clothing. Obviously, with large dogs, the paw alert is not appropriate for a DAD for children. However, for smaller dogs, a paw tap may be an acceptable alert, and may be more recognizable than a nose nudge. Most small dogs stand up and give a slight patter with both feet, as a little "soft dig".

Small dogs may be trained to stand and give a "soft dig" alert with their paws

- A common and effective alert for a medium to large sized dog is a **nudge** (or poke) with the nose, and we will give instructions for training this alert. This alert is generally easy to train, good for getting attention, can be used in virtually all settings, and is non-disruptive. This is the alert we most commonly recommend for DADs.

In the "Nudge" alert, the dog pokes the handler with his nose

There are teams who find something else to be best for them. The important thing to remember is that the dog also has a say in what will work best. It is very difficult to insist on something that you want but that the dog absolutely hates. The Nudge will be the example here. Other alerts will progress similarly. Work on this in a fun manner just as you would teach a trick. The alert must be something the dog has enjoyed learning all the way to reliability.

Training the Nudge
The *Nudge* is a nose push on your body with the mouth closed and no feet involved.

1. **Present the dog with a target,** such as a small (no more than two inches diameter) plastic lid, sticky note or duct tape, one to two feet in front of your dog's nose, **and wait for the dog to come to it to check it out**. As the dog is within an inch of it, or touching it, C/T. (If your dog lunges and tries to bite the target, C/T him as soon as he moves towards the target, before he can open his mouth. You may have to play around with placement of the target, moving it higher or placing it on a vertical

surface or the body sometimes helps, to make it so he cannot bite the target. Then gradually C/T closer approaches without opening the mouth.)

2. **Move the target toward your leg** in small increments, so that it finally is resting at dog nose height on your leg. This may take a session or two, depending on each of you. The goal is for the dog to enjoy touching the target, so there is no need to rush to the leg before the dog is successfully making contact with the target each time.

3. If necessary, **train your dog to push harder, so you can easily feel the nudge.** Stepping backwards slightly as your dog approaches can help with this, or you can just shape a harder nudge by only clicking harder and harder touches.

4. When the dog is reliably touching the target at your leg, you can **begin to add the verbal cue (e.g., "Nudge" or "Poke").** This is also when you will begin to make the target smaller to **begin fading the need for the target.** You can trim the target to a smaller size, and you also can use round sticky dots stuck to your pant leg. (If using colored dots, avoid the red ones until you are about to remove the dot entirely. That is a color that dogs see the least.) Also move the location of the target to different places on your leg (keep it at nose level), so he doesn't always touch the same place.

The goal in this step is to pair the cue while beginning to fade the target. This is a compound step so take your time and keep it fun. Proceed only when the target is faded and the cue is making sense to the dog. At this stage you should be able to point to your leg and ask for a nudge with your cue and get one. Congratulations, you have helped the dog understand the way a BG event will be communicated.

5. **Ask for random nudges throughout the day** when you are not having a training session. Just do one or two and then go on about your day. Change your position when asking for the nudge, so the dog will nudge you from the side, with your back turned and when you are seated.

   This is easy and fun to add in when you are just playing with the dog. For instance, if you are throwing a toy for your dog, when he brings it back, occasionally ask for a nudge before you throw it again. Don't do it every time, but let him realize that it's a fun behavior and you could ask for it at any time. Just keep your requests random, or you will teach the dog that the nudge is before or after another behavior. We will do that very soon and don't want to have to break apart something the dog had chained together by mistake.

Note — If you are training the small dog "dig," the progression is the same except you are encouraging a dual paw rat-a-tat behavior instead of the nose push. You may also have to begin while sitting on the floor. Do get into an upright position by step three.

Watch for —The dog will quite possibly begin to offer the alert behavior during the day for attention. This is a good sign, but it needs to be handled in such a way as to prevent him from thinking it works to solicit attention. *When you have not asked for the behavior, do not respond to it.* Just carry on with what you were doing. You can smile if you wish, but don't give any treats or verbal praise. It's a fine line as you don't want to discourage the actual behavior, but you want it only when you ask for it at this point.

Signals

It is important that the dog is able to indicate whether your BG is heading in a low or a high direction. This can be very useful information, even if you use a BG meter or CGM. As we mentioned earlier, these devices have a permitted level of inaccuracy (up to 20%) and can fail. They also give static information — they tell you what your BG is now or which way it has been trending recently.

The experience of DAD users over the years indicates that dogs can detect drops or rises in BG *ahead of the meter*, often by 15-30 minutes. This means that, even when your meter indicates that your BG is in the normal range, dogs can signal you if you are headed out of that range, permitting you to treat yourself more quickly and accurately. Training an alert plus low/high signals can help you keep your BG in a tighter range over time.

The choice of the signal behaviors is less constrained than the alert due to the fact that the dog already has your attention. Again, we suggest that the signals not be complicated or disruptive. Some of the common choices for a medium sized or larger dog are as simple as a **Sit, Down, Bow**, and even a **Paw-up** as a "high-five." Another option is to teach the dog to **Push the handler's hand** upward or downward (or Nudge the right or left hand) when the hand is presented after the alert is recognized.

Your training job will be easiest if you **pick behaviors that are easy for your dog to do.** To those of you who choose to use a Sit and a Down, they will no doubt be on a verbal cue already. That makes it sound easy, but don't assume that to be true. Some dogs find it quite confusing to use Sit and Down in another context. It is also crucial that you be able to recognize which signal means "low" and which signal means "high!" So be sure to choose signals that are distinct and make some sense to you, so that you can interpret them even when mentally impaired due to low or high BG.

Whatever the choice of the signal, **work to make sure that the dog responds quickly to the verbal cue** (not a hand signal) reliably, in any environment and under distracting circumstances. Work on these two signal behaviors in completely different sessions from any scent alert work. Keep the signal training very lighthearted and as much fun as teaching any trick.

II. Imprinting low BG scent

The process of imprinting your dog on low or high BG scent involves exposing him to the target odor, and rewarding him for detecting it. This step typically goes very quickly, and then it is time to add the alert behavior. *Do not begin working with scent until the alert behavior will happen any time you give a verbal cue in your training environment.* Pushing to the scent before having a solid alert behavior will only cause failure and confusion in the future steps.

Contrary to common belief, the imprinting does not have to be done over and over. Since the dog has no doubt already sensed the odor by living with you, this is not a new and novel smell. The goal in the imprinting process is simply to let him know that particular odor is important to you and has a paycheck involved.

Important Note — Check your BG prior to scent training. If you are much out of range, or are high, do not train with low scent. This is critical so that you are not presenting the dog with a combination of scents rather than just the target scent. If you are high, it is best not to work the dog on low scent until you are within normal range or are slightly low. Also, you will be less mentally aware or quick when you are experiencing a severe low (or high), and that foggy situation makes it difficult for you to be accurate with your timing in marking behaviors that help the dog understand what he did right.

We also advise that you review this chapter completely prior to beginning, so you have a full understanding of progression.

1. **Thaw your (closed) scent sample** for at least five minutes.

2. **Set the open sample at dog-nose level or below** in a location that prevents retrieval by the dog. This can be in a container with an open top such as a basket, lodged between two items, or even held in the hand of a helper in

a non-obvious manner. The sample container (tube) should not be easily seen by the dog. Have the dog out of the area while you set this up, so he cannot see the location of the sample. Do not work in an area with a strong draft or in front of a fan. The goal is to let the dog notice the scent, not to blow it all around the room so it is everywhere.

The scent sample can be placed in an open container, such as a cinder block, and the dog allowed to investigate.

3. **Watch your dog for signs of scent recognition.** Bring your dog into the area and watch your dog *closely*! Let the dog happen on the scent rather than pushing it toward him or leading him to it. You will see the dog tune into the scent (discovery), probably before coming right up to it. It is *not necessary* for the dog to put his nose on the sample. If the dog tunes into the scent at six to twelve inches away, that is well and good. You will see an indication that the dog has tuned in with nose motion, breathing change, head turn, ear motion, etc. Each dog has a style, but you will learn by watching closely and you will recognize when the dog has caught the scent. (We advise that you observe your dog in everyday activity, such as a walk. Learn what body language the dog displays when he finds a scent interesting. This will

help you in determining when he has recognized the target sample scent.)

4. **Click the dog at the very *instant* of recognition** and have the dog come *to you* for a treat. We want the dog to return to the handler so the treat happens there.

5. **Walk a short distance away and reapproach the sample** from a slightly different direction. Watch your dog and C/T when he recognizes the scent. Repeat this approach *up to* four times and then stop. This imprinting is done in very short numbers of repetitions on purpose. The dog will have a nose full of scent and there is no value in continuing to repeat this over and over again.

Imprinting is done for only three sessions and then is considered complete. Dogs learn scents easily and do not seem to forget them.

III. Training the alert chain

The **alert chain** is the foundation behavior that produces a reliable alert dog. What is a chain? Just like the term implies, it is a series of behaviors that are linked together in sequence to form a whole new behavior. Think of the dog who plays fetch. It looks like one behavior but actually is five skills (go to – pick up – hold – come – drop) linked together to become smooth enough to create a new behavior. We will teach the dog to perform the alert chain when he detects the low (or high) BG scent. This new chain is:

Dog *recognizes* scent → You *cue* a *nudge* → Dog *performs* nudge → C/T

There are a few concepts that are central to this training:

Scent is a *cue* to alert

Searching is not part of a medical alert dog's necessary skills – recognizing and informing is what we are after. You are not creating a search dog that must pinpoint the scent source and take you to it.

You are creating a tattletale who comes and notifies you when it senses the low BG scent. The scent is a *cue* to perform the alert chain, and we want the dog to expect the cue to emanate from a human. This is a very important difference and one that you must keep in mind throughout the training of the alert chain. It can be difficult to grasp the idea of scent acting as a cue (like the words "Sit" or "Down"), but scent cues are natural and easy for dogs to learn.

Human as scent source
With the successful imprinting complete, it is time to move the scent sample to the human. ***The scent sample should be placed on a person for all training going forward*** (except during initial signal training), until the dog is reliably alerting/signaling in most situations, and you have moved on to "Training Games" (see Chapter 9).

Put the thawed scent sample on yourself or on a helper. Do not make the container obvious to the dog. Hold it in your loosely closed hand, put it in a pocket or sleeve, in a pant leg or tucked in the top of your sock or boot. Cargo pants pockets are wonderful for this work. Just have the scent located where the dog will be able to sense it easily. Placing it near nose level or below will make the beginning exercises easier for him. You want the scent to escape well but you need to avoid making the source obviously visible to the dog. You do not want him to believe he must *see* the source. This work is about recognizing solely with the nose.

The human scent source (you or a helper) needs to remain fairly still but not obviously stiff. Moving about excessively will create a sizeable scent pool and it will be difficult for you to watch closely or know just when the dog recognizes the scent. Keeping things simple in the beginning will allow you to progress at a faster rate. There will be plenty of time to test limits later. Right now your goal is to explain to the dog that *low scent is a cue* to respond — nothing more and nothing less.

Training guidelines
Work one session a day, five days per week. You can work two sessions a day if you wish, but keep them short and separate them so the dog doesn't have a nose full of scent before you begin.

Work an alert chain session with the goal of three to five nice repetitions. If you get three great alerts and then the dog is less motivated, stop and do another session at a later time. This is a learning process that involves teaching a response to an olfactory stimulus while also creating motivation. The sessions must be exciting and fun for the dog, there is no benefit in boring him with the process.

Training steps
1. **Place the closed, but thawed, low scent sample on yourself** or a helper without the dog watching the process. Work in a low distraction area.

2. **Prepare by asking for a Nudge** (or other alert behavior) and C/T. The purpose for the cued alert is to set the tone for the session. Disengage from the dog for a moment so it is less obvious that you are progressing to the next step of opening the scent sample.

3. **Open the scent sample** (quietly) and **let the dog recognize the scent** on his own while you are watchful. If the dog stares at you, do not return direct eye contact. Just avert your eyes (not your head position) slightly so you can watch the dog but he is not being rewarded with your complete attention.

   Patience is often required. Expect the first few trials of this to have variable timing on your part. Relax — you and the dog are learning this together — you will both make a few mistakes. You will do much better if you just take it easy and make it lighthearted fun.

4. **The *instant* you see recognition of the scent source, give your verbal cue for the alert.** C/T for the alert. In fact, have a party!

   It is common for a dog to want a little encouragement when they recognize the scent. If they seem to need that, make your cue to alert very upbeat. It can also be effective to praise or say "Yes" at the scent recognition and then cue the alert. Do not add this if the dog doesn't seem to require it. Adding things that you will have to fade away later is a step to choose only if necessary. A simple rule of thumb is to use the help three times and then try the sequence without it (as removing the "Yes" and just giving the alert cue, or giving only the "Yes" and waiting for the alert without a verbal cue).

5. **Change your position slightly**, by turning a bit or stepping aside one step, and repeat Step 4. Don't create a huge scent pool by wandering all around the area. The goal is three to five successful reps.

6. The routine will become fast and easy for both of you. **Begin changing your starting position and change your location** in the room you are working in as well. All changes must be slight and following the 80%+ Rule will keep you from moving too fast for the dog. You are establishing a pattern that will be paramount for your alert dog.

7. **Begin to fade the verbal cue for the alert. At this point, the alert should be quite smooth and reliable.** Beginning to fade the verbal cue is best done randomly. Do two reps and then see if the dog is inclined to offer the alert without hearing the alert cue immediately.

   In the fading process, you don't simply remove the cue entirely and never use it again. Use it randomly or when necessary. The important part of establishing the alert behavior is in getting an *immediate* response when the dog recognizes that scent is present. If your dog is beginning to take more time or hesitate before giving the alert, go back to cuing the alert for a few sessions, and then proceed forward again. Give some thought also to whether or not you are creating motivation with happy praise and valued rewards. The dog must remain motivated to alert. Your joy with his success means everything to the dog. Keep the game fun and interesting.

Note — The goal for training at this point should be *scent causes alert* — no prompts. Expect this to take at least one to two weeks to become reliable before moving to the next phase of the chain (signals). We prefer that there is no need for any verbal cue prior to training the next portion of the chain. This is the foundation for the rest of the structure, so it needs to be solid.

IV. Adding the low and high signals

When your dog is proficient at offering the alert behavior with the low BG odor (with minimal cuing), it's time to start training signal behaviors in response to the low and high scents. Typically this new behavior establishes very quickly. The dog is already familiar with the scents, so adding a known position or trick is simple for him.

Be sure you have your low and high signals well trained and reliable on verbal cues before progressing to this step. This new step will be fun for the dog because it's simple and moves fairly fast. Dogs love fast paced games!

Introducing the Signals
1. **Thaw a low and a high scent sample.** You can use two like items to conceal the scent sources. Examples would be plastic containers, cardboard boxes, or empty flower pots, all of which can be upside down to cover the scent tubes and hopefully cannot be picked up and taken away as a toy. You also do not want the covers to be so airtight that scent will not escape readily. It is also possible to use two people with scent planted on them, but keep in mind

that they themselves should have blood glucose in normal range.

2. **Set up the two sources** about six feet apart. Let them sit for about three minutes before beginning the next step.

3. **Expose your dog to low and high scents and cue the signals.** You may wish to have your dog on a leash for the first exercise, so you are able to keep them focused. That is optional but do not let him wander all around the area or from one to the other source at this time.

   A. Walk with your dog directly to the low source. As you get within eight inches of the source, stop and cue your dog with the **low signal** you have taught. C/T for the correct signal, and give a big reward. At this time, the dog does not have to give you the regular alert. If the dog insists, acknowledge it with praise but do not C/T until after he gives the cued signal.

   B. Walk away from the two scent sources. **Repeat** this once again with the low source. Walk away from both sources.

   C. Repeat this same procedure with the high source, cuing the **high signal** you have taught as a trick. Do this twice as you did for the low scent.

   D. Take a minute break and walk the dog a little distance away to clear the nose and the mind. Return and with this pass walk to the **low, cue the signal, reward — walk to the high source and cue the signal, reward**. End the session at this point.

Notes — Do not expect perfection in this first session. Remember, it's not a new scent to the dog, but giving a signal is new. If the dog is a bit flustered, don't worry about that. This is both exciting and different from the normal alert pattern so it will feel odd to both of you.

This will be a sequence that you may find yourself going back to on occasion to help sort out precise signal skills. Feel free to repeat this as necessary throughout the dog's career, just to keep the signal behaviors polished. Our only warning is that you do not create searching for scent. For that reason, working the sequence with people as the scent sources is preferred.

Training the low alert/signal chain
1. **Set up only the low source this time**. As the dog recognizes the scent, raise up both hands in a motion as if to mime a "What's up?" as you verbally cue the low signal. C/T for the low signal. Walk away and repeat this three to a maximum of five times. Take a good break.

The "What's up?" gesture acknowledges the alert and asks the dog for the low/high signal.

Note — This physical motion by you will become very important to the dog. This is how you will ask for the signal after the alert. It is also an indication to the dog that you recognized the alert! Recognition of the alert becomes critical for the dog, as when the diabetic is significantly out of range, they are mentally foggy and often miss an alert. The dog has no way of knowing you understood the alert for sure unless he receives recognition. This signal by you is both recognition of the alert and permission to continue by giving the signal. Here is the vital communication portion of the alert chain between the dog and the handler.

2. After a several minute break, **put the low scent source on yourself** as has been previously done, get the alert (it is fine to cue it if necessary) and raise your hands in the "What's up?" motion and cue the signal. The instant you get the signal, C/T and have a party! Repeat this at least three times and stop for sure if you have done five repetitions.

The new chain sequence is now:

Dog *detects scent*
↓
Dog *alerts*
↓
You give "What's up?" motion while cuing signal
↓
Dog *performs* **signal**
↓
C/T

You may find that the dog needs a "Yes" from you prior to you asking "What's up?" for a few reps. Not all dogs will need that, but many like to know they did right by alerting. If you use this, do fade it quickly as you want the "What's up?" to be the important link to the rest of the chain. Also, as this sinks in a bit, you can give the "What's up?" motion while asking "What's up?" verbally, so the dog will understand either method of recognition. This is easiest if you add it as you are fading the signal verbal cue. The final chain will go like this:

Scent recognition → Alert → "What's up?" → Signal → C/T

Congratulations! You have completed the alert chain for the low scent.

We advise that you work with this complete chain until you are able to fade some of the cues and the chain is feeling more comfortable for you and the dog. Don't rush to get to the high scent chain. Remember, you have added several new things to the mix, with the acknowledgement/question "What's up?" motion and verbal that you give at the alert behavior and also a signal to indicate that the scent is low. Let this all settle in and become smooth enough that it flows quickly from one part to the next.

Be thrilled with the dog's work so that his motivation is encouragement by you as well as a good reward (paycheck). Follow the 80%+ Rule faithfully. That means fading verbal cues should not be too abrupt. Rushing at this point will cause failures in the future and serious backstepping to rebuild a smooth chain.

Adding the high signal
This is **a return to Step 2 of "Training the low alert/signal chain"** but with the use of high scent. With a high scent source hidden on you, acknowledge the alert with "What's up?" and cue the signal after the alert. This addition will go much more quickly than it did with the low scent. You already have the full chain working for the low so simply cuing the high signal at the end of the chain is very easy.

Continue to work on the alert chain with both high or low scent so that the dog does not need additional cues from you to complete the task.

V. Generalization

We mentioned in the overview section that the process requiring the most time and diligence would be the generalizing. Perhaps it will help you if you understand a bit about how dogs learn compared to humans.

A human child will learn to perform a task (e.g., stacking blocks) and can immediately do it in any room of the house. Dogs do not learn that way — they learn through association. This means they are place learners. They associate a behavior with all that is happening as it's learned. This can be valuable, but means you must also vary your training location *as the behavior becomes more reliable.* By working in the same place until a behavior is happening in a dependable fashion, you increase the dog's ability to concentrate on the learning process without distraction.

To aid the dog in furthering the dependability of these new alert behaviors, you need to begin branching out. This doesn't mean you are moving from the family room to the grocery store in one big trip! Here again we have a little rule of thumb to follow:

- Work the behavior in a **familiar place.**

- As the dog is successful there, **add a distraction.** This can simply be a noise, another person, a toy within vision or held in your hand.

- As the dog becomes successful with distractions, you can **move to a new place** without distractions.

- And so it goes — familiar place without distraction, add distraction, then to new place without distraction.

As you move to public places, you cannot control all situations regarding distractions. (Just as an aside, motion is a huge distraction.) If the dog is overwhelmed, try to gain some distance from a big distraction. Gaining distance from the distraction can be very valuable.

With time and many trials and successes, you will see that the dog is becoming more and more reliable in new situations. If you seem to be having many failures, step back a bit with the difficulty of the circumstances. Training a reliable partner is all about repeating many successful patterns and avoiding the repeating of failures.

Alerting during daily activities

Simple things like changing your position can throw your dog off track. This was mentioned in the alert training section. We encouraged you to get the alert when standing, sitting and even lying down. Now you will have to remember that you may be moving, typing at the computer, washing dishes, folding laundry, and various other activities in your normal day. The dog must feel comfortable interrupting you no matter what you are doing!

We suggest you make a list and work through it. Places are also important, as in the bathroom or shower. So, jot down all the places and positions you could be in when the dog detects scent and work a few sessions in each. The dog will find this fun as it gives variety to something he is good at. Always be thrilled that he alerted. You are helping build confidence so that the dog will not hesitate when there is a BG event.

During all these position and place sessions, you may find the dog occasionally reluctant to alert. Go ahead and cue him so he understands that you *do* want to know. This is why we wanted a verbal cue on all the parts of the chain. When the dog needs a little encouragement, that familiar cue will get the job done. Don't overdo or keep helping more than necessary, but you are partners and help goes both ways.

Moving alerts

Do some moving alert sessions in a very comfortable and familiar place with the dog. Walk *very* slowly, and cue the dog to give you the alert cue from the back, side and front. This is difficult at first and you can practice it without any scent. It can be helpful to walk in a stepwise fashion, hesitating at first to allow the dog to do the alert while you are briefly stationary. This is just to help the dog realize that he can perform the alert behavior with you in motion. As the dog becomes familiar with that, then you can incorporate some motion in your regular training sessions using scent.

Practice getting the nudge alert from the side while you are moving...

...and from the back.

Many dogs are confused at first with just how to get your attention when you are in motion and you may see slight variation of the alert. An example would be a dog that comes to your front to give a nudge, to make sure he has succeeded. It is important to find what works for you and the dog without too much deviation from the trained alert behavior.

Real-time lows and highs

Now that you have a reliable alert chain you can take advantage of all the spontaneous lows and highs that you provide as the human scent source.

When your BG is low or high and your dog has not yet reacted to it, just be casual and walk him through the alert. Breathe toward the dog. Do not blow a blast of air toward the dog's face as if you were blowing out candles. Simply exhale softly near his head (as if saying "ah" without the audible). As the dog recognizes or looks at you, cue the alert and the signal and then have a party. Never repeat more than one more rep per BG event. You are simply helping the dog generalize the alert chain to real life.

Spontaneous alerts

You may have already noticed the dog performing the alert behavior spontaneously when your BG was out of range. This is always a very exciting event! But if this hasn't happened yet, this does not mean that the dog doesn't "get it." There are many small details involved in a beautiful and flawless alert, many of which pertain to the human portion of the responsibility.

The handler that is in an out-of-range BG situation is naturally a bit foggy. So it's very common for a handler to miss many of those first alerts. The handler is also not expecting an alert subconsciously so they often go unnoticed. It is also common for the dog to be less sure of himself so the alert is much softer and easily mistaken for something else. This is due to the fact that you are not in a training session and all prepared as usual. When the dog gives a soft alert then receives no acknowledgement, he is often not inclined to repeat and be pushy.

With this in mind, you will need to try hard to notice the alert behavior and ask if there is an issue ("What's up?"). You will also have to be careful not to reward before verifying with a meter or CGM check. There will be times that you show normal and in those situations it is wise to test again in about 20 minutes. Do give some interaction but avoid heavy rewarding of the unknown at this stage. If you are out of range when you retest, cue the alert chain and reward heavily!

When a dog begins real alerts is an individual thing that varies vastly with each team. As a team, you and the dog both contribute to the success. You have responsibility in being receptive, patient and a full partner in the process. **When dogs fail to perform what they have learned it is not a dog failure but one of the team.** Dogs are no more perfect in the beginning than humans are when learning something new. You have worked hard to master a behavior chain — but you are still working with a living being and not a machine. We think that's the best part — getting to work with a creature that thinks and cares. There will be hits and misses. With time and patience, it all comes together.

Chapter 7

Car alerts

If you drive, you will want to train your DAD to alert while you are driving. There are a few special considerations in training car alerts, due to the physical confines of the space, the position of the dog, a need to safely get your attention, etc. It may also be necessary to teach your dog that he can and should alert you while the car is moving, and show him how best to do it. Here are some considerations and suggestions:

Position in car

Where does your dog ride in the car? Wherever it is, he needs to be comfortable and safe, and not interfere with your ability to drive safely. We do not advise having a dog ride in the front seat or loose in the car. Deploying airbags can fatally injure a dog in the front seat. Your dog need not be in your lap, or even in the front seat with you, in order to detect your BG changes, and will likely be safer riding behind you. This can be in the back seat or further back, whichever is practical and comfortable, and can be on the seat or the floor. Consider the use of a doggy seat belt or crate for safety.

Alerts and signals

How your dog rides in the car will determine whether or not he can alert you in the way you have trained (nudge, paw, etc.). If behind you in a small car, he may be able to alert you by touching your shoulder or arm. If he cannot easily reach you, or is uncomfortable doing so while the car is moving, you will need to train an alternative alert. Similarly, depending on the signals you have trained, he may not be able to signal your low or high in the car (and/or it may not be safe for you to take your eyes off the road to watch his signal). Since you should stop driving and check your BG after your dog alerts, you can either ask for the signal then, or just go with what the meter indicates.

Training a car alert

If you will be using the alert you have already trained, you may need to show your dog how to perform the behavior while in the car. **We cannot emphasize enough how important it is to make safety your priority anytime you are in a car!** Train this first while stationary, then while moving, always keeping safety in mind. Training is always secondary. Do not attempt to train while in traffic, and if your dog alerts while you are driving, you must stop the vehicle before rewarding or checking your BG. We highly recommend having your trainer or another person help with this.

1. **Practice the alert without scent** to warm your dog up on the behavior and figure out how it will work in the car. With the car stationary, point to where you want your dog to nudge or paw (go back to using a target if necessary), cue the alert and C/T for a nice alert. Be sure the dog can easily do a noticeable cued alert in this position before moving on.

2. **Use scent to cue the alert** by opening a scent source and waiting for recognition and alert. Verbally cue the alert if needed and C/T for the alert. Since the scent will fill the car quickly, you will only be able to do a few reps of this before stopping. Train low BG scent separately from high BG scent.

3. In a safe location, such as a large, quiet parking lot, **practice getting the alert while driving.** Start driving slowly, then repeat Step 2. A helper can be critical here for training and safety.

4. **Generalize the behavior** by training in many safe locations.

Alternative alerts

It may not be possible or practical for your dog to give his normal alert in the car (especially if he rides in the cargo area or in a crate), or he may not feel comfortable doing so. In this case, it can be helpful to train an alternative alert using a bell or other sound-producing device. There are many devices currently available, but some possibilities include:

- **Pet-2-Ring™ Doorbell system** (http://www.pet2ring.com/). This provides a large button for the dog to push and the bell itself is up front where you can easily hear it. This button can be mounted satisfactorily on nearly every car, either on the floor or the seat, or on the side of a dog crate.

Dogs can be taught to press a bell to alert in the car. Shown is the Pet-2-Ring™ Doorbell system.

- **Battery-operated remote door-bells**. You will probably need to modify the button to make it large enough for your dog to easily activate it.

- Sound-producing **push-buttons,** such as the "Easy Button™" (Staples(R) store).

You will train this just as you have for the normal alert, except that instead of nudging or pawing you, you will direct the dog to nudge or paw the button. It can be easiest to train this first in your house, then move the button to the car. Be sure to mount the button in a location that makes it easy for your dog to activate it, at nose level (for the nudge alert).

Checking before driving

Hopefully, you are already checking your BG before attempting to drive a car. Your dog can be helpful here in indicating if you are headed up or down in BG. Practice opening the scent just before putting your dog in the car, to ensure that he can alert and signal just before entering the car. Before driving, be sure to expose your dog to your breath by talking to him, etc. as you are loading him into the car, and pay attention to any interest or alerts you may get.

Chapter 8

Night alert training

Although some dogs will spontaneously offer nighttime alerts, that is considered the exception. Most dogs need some training to accomplish reliability in this critical area. Once again, it is important to understand what we are asking of the dog and how the dog learns.

We are asking the dog to wake himself up and alert you if you go out of normal range. Yet all work up to this point has been with the dog in an awake state. Neither dogs nor humans are as alert while sleeping as they are when awake. There is that little subconscious part of us that can sense something at times, yet we can also sleep right through many situations.

We have been training the dog's conscious mind to sense a scent and perform a behavior. The subconscious mind hasn't been involved in this work up to now. It's time to begin to spur a response that will cause the dog to wake and alert out of a sleep state for scent just as he would for a bright light or unusual noise.

Preparation training: Interrupted play

This fast-paced and fun game helps the dog learn to notice the scent cue even when focusing on another engaging activity. We have found this technique to be key in accomplishing reliable night alerts. Dependable alerts during the day with heavy distraction also benefit greatly from this play-training game. So, don't skip this step only to have to go back and do it later. Remember, the goal with all the training steps is to develop a very reliable alert dog in all situations.

Choose a game that the dog enjoys playing with you. A game of tug works well, as you can maintain control of the state of the game and cut it off easily. You will have to be quick with this game, because dogs love this and are much faster than we are.

Use a toy that you can move around in a tease fashion near the ground and entice the dog to join in. Play a bit, and in one of those quick moments while the dog is catching a breath, you can wave your hand with a scent source past the dog while you retrieve the toy back from play and put it behind your back quickly, while giving the verbal cuc to alcrt. The dog may respond immediately or look completely confused. Be ready to help him out if necessary. After you get the alert (you do not have to get the whole chain in these first few reps), immediately go back to playing the game.

The goal is to get in a good five reps that break up the game momentarily for an alert and yet do not stop all the fun completely. You will have much more success with this in a non-distracting environment to start. However, do generalize the game to other environments with distractions. Ultimately, you will want the dog to interrupt play with someone else and even with another dog.

Night alerts sessions

Once you are getting solid, quick alerts during interrupted play exercises you may begin night alert training.

You will need a dog who is ready for a nap. Anticipate when the dog may be resting so that you have a scent source ready to use. Too much action in going to get a scent tube will probably wake up the dog and we do want him sleeping.

While the dog is sleeping, open the scent tube and slowly and quietly wave it past the dog's head. Wait for an indication that the dog received scent. You may see his nose twitch very slightly, or the dog may wake and raise his head. Each dog is slightly different, but what you are after is that slight recognition that you have watched for in early training. When you see that, immediately cue the alert chain.

You will not be able to get in many repetitions of this training as the dog will become aware and will not be asleep. Work to get two or three reps some time apart (with the dog dozing off in between) and then stop. Do this several times a week and work at different times of the day. You need the dog to wake in the daytime when he is asleep as well as nighttime. Remember to change your position, so that you are seated, reclining or laying down when the dog alerts.

Some dogs initially may be unresponsive to the scent while sleeping, and need a more graduated training approach. Try timing your first sessions for when the dog is just getting sleepy, beginning to doze off, or sleeping lightly due to environmental conditions (noises, etc.), to make it easier for him to awaken to the scent. You can also try gently touching the sleeping dog, or making a quiet noise, to get him out of deep sleep. As he becomes more responsive to the scent over time, work towards training when he is sleeping more soundly.

As this behavior becomes more solid, and only then, occasionally be unresponsive to the first alert. Let the dog get pushy about waking you up. You may find that he improvises a bit with the trained alert behavior. This is not to be discouraged unless it is harmful to you physically. The dog is working to get your attention — be sure he can alert at a level that will wake you from deep sleep.

If you have an opportunity to practice in a strange place, such as a family member's home, do so. The dog will quickly sort out that the job is the same no matter where you are located.

Sound alerts

If you have a small dog, or find that your dog's daytime alert is not sufficient to wake you when sleeping, you may wish to train him to alert by ringing a bell or alarm. This may also be the best approach for a dog who needs to wake the parents of a diabetic child in another room. Instructions for this can be found in the chapter on Car Alerts.

Chapter 9

Training games

Use these games to refine your dog's alerting skills during training. Remember to be ready to help your dog out, by cueing the alert/signal behaviors, if he seems tentative or does not offer the behaviors on his own.

Hurry up – This is to help with slow initial alerts. When the dog recognizes the scent and is starting to alert, back up a few quick steps to encourage him to come to you faster.

Hide and surprise – Have the scent tube with you, but closed up. Either sit or lie down with the dog on a down nearby. Do not put the dog on a stay, just a calm "settle." Out of the dog's vision, take the top from the scent tube and hide it on yourself so it isn't in plain view, but the scent can release. This will help with generalizing positions.

Where did that come from? –When the dog is out of the room, hide the scent tube and go about what you were doing. Just wait and see how and when the dog recognizes the scent and alerts. This is a wonderful way to judge reliability outside of training sessions.

Chair it is – Hide the scent source on a chair near nose level. You can then work on sitting near the chair, standing by the chair, or walking around the chair as separate sessions to help generalize human positions while alerting.

Walking surprise – This is like the hide and surprise, except you are walking. Open the closed scent tube without having it in view and watch for a gesture that the dog recognizes scent. This is difficult, so walk slowly at first and be realistic with your expectations of success. A little help, in the form of showing the dog where to alert, may be in order.

Eyes or nose? – Put out 2 and then eventually up to 5 items (scent tubes for one) but only one is a scent source. The others are virgin.

You can arrange them in a small circle or in a line up, but put at least 12 inches to 14 inches between them. Let the dog indicate which one is positive and reward. You can work this with the whole alert chain including signals, or you can shorten it to a fast paced game of hot and cold.

Uncooperative – When the dog is **_reliable_** with the alert, become stubborn and ignore the first or second alert. If your dog offers a repeated alert, click and reward generously! If not, be prepared to cue the repeated alert. This is to simulate what happens in the real world. We want the dog to be insistent and if unable to get a response, to go tell someone else (have someone else available if you are going to push it that far).

Scent maintenance games

Practice games for generalizing various alert situations. As always, be prepared to help your dog out if he is confused or tentative. Keep the games fun and easy, so that the dog enjoys being successful and builds confidence. It is easy to make a game harder, but remember, you are **_training – not testing!!_** If scent work is made to be too serious, it will simply be a job. Don't create a discouraged worker's attitude in your dog. Feel free to make up your own games as well – your dog will love you for it!

Find the positive – This game uses a box (a sizeable cardboard box with low sides) and "stuff" in it, along with a scent source. Set the box down and let the dog check it out. Watch closely for little signs of when the dog recognized the scent. Depending on how reliable the alert is, you may click then and have the dog come to you for a reward, or you can wait for an alert and then reward.

Which box? – This is a variation on the above game, and simply adds other boxes. At first they can all be positive. As the dog learns, this game can be fun with only one positive. It is very helpful to have all the boxes hold the same "stuff" but only one contains a positive scent source.

Shell game – This game is similar to the regular shell game, except that you are using a scent sample and you must realize that there will be residual scent left in each place. This teaches the dog to find the "strongest" scent. Be careful to place the positive cover (box, napkin, whatever) in a new place and move the negative covers to new places as well. If a dog tells you about the old place, acknowledge it but only give the big reward for the actual source. It is best to use only two or three covers and not to move things too rapidly. Be sure and leave at least a foot of distance between each cover.

Catch me alert – Hide a scent source and begin to walk a circle. Keep walking the circle while the dog seeks out the scent. The goal is to have the dog alert you while you are moving. If the dog is not ready for this level, you can take a step and then hesitate and then take another step, like an old-style "down the aisle" movement.

Chapter 10

Additional skills

Depending on your circumstances, you may wish to train your dog to do additional tasks to assist you. These should be taught only AFTER the alert and signal training is complete, and your dog is able to alert you to changes in your BG in most environments. This is not an exhaustive list of possibilities, just some of the most common tasks our clients use. If other skills are needed, work with your trainer to teach your dog what you need him to do.

Third-party alerts/Go for help

This task trains the dog to go find someone (other than the diabetic), give the alert to that person, then lead the person to the diabetic handler. Like the initial alert training, this is a behavior chain. It is helpful for all DADs to have this skill, and essential for any dog paired with a young child. Often, dogs will spontaneously offer this behavior if the diabetic is unresponsive to the alert, but it is valuable to train it formally as well. The foundation of this behavior is a good recall ("Come"), so be sure your dog has this skill before proceeding. You will also need a helper for this training.

When trained, this sequence is:

Dog detects low/high BG scent
↓
(Diabetic/handler directs dog to "Find help")
↓
Dog goes to third party and alerts
↓
(Third party asks dog to "Show me" and return to handler)

(Steps in parentheses are optional, depending on your situation.)

Foundation skills:

- **Teach your dog to alert a "third party"** (your helper). Instruct your helper in how to cue your dog's alert and signals, and have them practice getting these behaviors, marking and rewarding them. No scent source is used in this practice.

- **Teach the dog to run to another person and back.** Both people have treats and clickers. Have your helper call the dog ("Come"), C/T when dog arrives. Handler immediately calls dog back, C/T when dog arrives. Practice a few rounds of this until dog easily goes back and forth between people (dogs typically love this game; it's also a great way to practice Come). You may notice the dog running toward the alternate person before being called. To keep the recall cue strong, call the dog back to you if he has not waited for the cue, so that he stays aware of the verbal cue.

Building the third-party alert chain:
We do this by "back-chaining" the steps of the sequence:

1. **Train return to the handler.** Helper takes dog a short distance (six to ten feet or so) from handler, says, "Show me" just before handler cues, "Come." Helper goes with dog to handler, where dog is rewarded. Practice until dog readily returns to handler on "Show me" cue.

2. **Train third-party alert and return to handler.** Repeat Step 1, with helper cueing the alert (without the signal at first) before saying, "Show me." Be sure to reward for the alert, and C/T the return to the handler.

3. **Train the dog to "Find help."** Open a scent sample on your body and wait for your dog to alert. As soon as he alerts you, say, "Find help" and have your helper call the dog ("Come") and cue the alert. The helper should reward the alert, then tell the dog to "Show me," and return to the handler for reward and praise.

4. **Practice and generalize the third-party alert.** Practice the chain until your dog readily leaves you to go to your helper when you say "Find help," and is fluent at alerting the other person. Then add distance in your house by having the helper move progressively further away from you, until they are in other rooms, outside, etc. Practice this outside your home, and in public places with increasing distractions. In addition, sometimes be unresponsive to your dog's alert, and hold off on saying "Find help," to teach the dog to leave you and alert another person if you are incapacitated and cannot give the cue.

Note – If you are training this alert for a child diabetic, you will want to introduce this task early in DAD alert training. The dog need not alert the child, but can be taught to immediately go to the parent (or other caregiver) and alert. Modify the alert/Go for Help training so that the BG scent cue directs the dog to go immediately to a third party to alert.

Retrieve blood glucose meter, juice box, glucose tablets, etc.

These tasks are all the same: retrieve a desired item on verbal or low/high BG scent cue. You will have the greatest success if you only train retrieval of a few essential items (more items = more confusion for the dog), and if these items are generally found in one or a few places in your home or elsewhere (so the dog does not have to search for them). For instance, if you need the dog to bring you glucose tablets, have containers available at all times on your nightstand, on a particular table in the living room, and on a low shelf in the kitchen.

Some people also train one or more of these retrieves as low/high BG signals. If you choose to do this, keep in mind that the retrieve item must be available at all times to the dog in order for him to signal you. We do not recommend this as a preferred signal.

Training a retrieve is complex, and there are several ways to do it. We have listed resources containing instructions for possible approaches in the Appendix. Work with your trainer on one of these methods to train the retrieve. As a final step, teach your dog to get a desired item by placing it in an accessible location and cueing the retrieve with a particular word (i.e., "Get meter" or just "Meter").

Finding/trailing the diabetic

This is primarily a skill for DADs who work for children, who may wander away from the dog/parents at home or out in public. Most dogs love this game! Again, your dog will need a good response to the "Come" cue before beginning this training.

1. **Teach the dog to find the diabetic.** You can start this game indoors or outside (in a safe location). Have the subject (diabetic) carry the dog's favorite reward (food or toy), and show it to the dog while a helper holds the dog back. The subject should tease the dog with the reward, then run away and duck out of sight. They may clap, whistle, etc. to excite the dog as they run away, if needed. Be sure the dog is focused on the subject as they disappear. As soon as they are out of sight, the helper should say, "Find Betty" (or whatever the subject's name is) and release the dog. The subject should praise and reward the dog as soon as he arrives.

   Repeat this exercise, with the subject going further and further away, a few times, but quit before the dog gets tired.

2. **Train the dog to find the subject without seeing her run away.** Set up as in Step 1, and run one trial with the dog seeing the subject hide. Then send the subject to hide, and turn the dog away (or cover his eyes) as the subject leaves and hides. Release the dog to "Find Betty," and have the subject reward the dog when found. Note: when moving to this step outdoors, help the dog learn to search with his nose (rather than visually) by having the subject hide up wind of where the dog will run. That way the dog is working into the scent, making it easier to recognize scent of the subject as she passes by, and follow his nose into the hiding location.

3. **Train a "cold" search**. After several days of training Step 2, have the subject hide (not too far away) without the dog knowing. Cue the dog to "Find Betty" and go with him, helping to reward when the subject is found.

Additional skills – If you feel that the diabetic may go far, and/or your dog moves so fast you can't keep up with him, you may wish to add the "Show me/Return to handler" as outlined above. Work to teach your dog to "ping-pong" between the subject and handler, until the two are together. Also, if you want to use this skill in public places (shopping malls, downtown, etc.), be sure to train it on leash after Step 3 is achieved. If more extensive tracking skills are required, there are numerous books available which specifically teach tracking.

Chapter 11

Troubleshooting

Every team is unique and will face small bumps along the training and working process, so we want to touch on the more common issues. **Remember, continued upkeep training is required to maintain alerting skills for all teams.** It is important to keep the training games fun for both you and the dog while remaining realistic in the goal to sustain a clean alert behavior and clear signals.

If you find you are getting occasional alerts rather than the 95% you hoped for, remember that the dog is now generalizing the behavior to everyday life. The real world has very few perfect percentages and beginning DAD's are no exception. It will be hit and miss for a while.

We strongly advise that you keep a very simple log and note the time of the day and what you and the dog were doing when you received an alert. Also note the same when you went out of range and did not receive an alert. Such information is invaluable in knowing what areas of training need revisiting. Usually there is an obvious area that has not been adequately generalized and requires a simple fix. Logs are critical information right at your fingertips. Example log forms are available electronically (see Appendix) and provided in the Appendix.

Missed alerts
It is extremely common for new teams to be convinced that there are many missed alerts. Quite typically, the dog is giving a soft alert and getting no response, or the handler is foggy and not anticipating an alert, so actually misses the more reserved alert behavior. This more reserved alert behavior is seen regularly when the team is in a new environment or under heavy distractions. Humans tend to want a very bold and repeated behavior that they can't miss. Consider that as the goal, but also be aware that you must pay close attention so you can determine that the dog is or is not communicating as desired.

If you feel there are many missed alerts, **refer to your log** and note whether there are some commonalities that would indicate some specific training area is weak. Those could be time of day, during certain situations or places, dependent on what you are doing at the time, etc.

When you have determined the likely weakness criteria, **go back and train** through that. We have seen many teams claim missed alerts, but find the dog is simply not confident that the alert behavior is desired under particular circumstances. Dogs don't care to make mistakes any more than we do, so a new dog may just need a bit of confidence building.

If you are a well-established team and are suddenly having missed alerts that were not a previous issue, look at your log but also have the dog examined to make sure there isn't a health issue. That simple log will give you many answers. Changes in the dog's environment, changes in the handler's health, new medications, etc. can be very significant. Reliable dogs do not abruptly stop working for no reason.

False alerts

This is a term that most often is simply a misunderstanding. The dog may have become successful at getting your attention in a way similar to the alert behavior because he receives something he wants – be it attention or even a reward of another type. As was mentioned in the *Training step-by-step* chapter, do not reward a modification of the alert behavior. If you are in doubt as to whether it is a weak alert, test and then test again in 15 minutes. The dog will not receive a reward unless the test shows there is a BG event. You can smile and acknowledge the dog, but refrain from heavy praise or full attention on him if you are in doubt. As the dog finds the modified behavior does not get the results he wants, it will fade away.

This brings up the point of choosing an alert behavior that is not something the dog does frequently to gain your attention. You do not want to have to guess whether or not you received an alert or a solicitation to play. The alert behavior needs to be specific and very discernible by you. If you get a slight deviation, ask the dog to alert with the cue again, and continue the chain from the proper alert.

If the dog has modified the alert behavior into something that you find less definitive, go back to that portion of the training and practice the alert without scent with the trained cue and clean it up.

Multiple alerts

Frequently a dog will continue giving alerts over and over, particularly with a high BG event as that can take a long time to come back into normal range. Naturally, you will be reluctant to not show appreciation for the alert, but it can become frustrating to be bothered again and again. We encourage you to teach a cutoff signal for the more determined dog, so he realizes that you are taking care of things and they can take a break for a bit.

Not all dogs continue to be assertive after they become seasoned with experience, but there are those individuals that do. Do not completely ignore the repeated alert, but do not reward it either. Instead, acknowledge it with a smile or "Thank you" that lets the dog know that you got the alert. You will also stop asking "What's up?" as you just did that a few minutes ago. If this doesn't prove sufficient to deal with your dog, do train the "Enough" signal outlined below.

"Enough" — Teach this as a trick to get the cue into the dog's vocabulary of words. It is a fun game for the dog, but one that requires you to be rather quick on your timing. No treats are required, nor do you need a clicker. The whole point of this game is to teach the dog that "Enough" is his cue to take a break.

Play by jazzing up the dog to interact with you (no toy is needed) and when he is interacting and having a great time, abruptly turn your back to him as you say "Enough." The dog will cease heavy interaction in a few seconds and at that point you abruptly turn back and begin playing again. Do this up to five times, each time stopping motion with the "Enough" cue and returning to play when the dog is not interacting. Returning to play is the reward. The dog will begin to stop play more and more quickly as that will get you to return to play sooner. While playing this game, you are introducing the cue to mean just what it says — enough.

"Got it" — a variation on the "Enough" cue is simply to always tell the dog you have things handled after receiving the complete alert chain, once you have tested and made the adjustments necessary with either the high or low BG treatment. The dog will watch this routine regularly and realize that you have responded to his information by giving him the "Got it" cue and done other typical things like adjusting the pump, having juice, etc. As good observers, many dogs sort this out on their own. However, there is no harm in giving the dog a cue to let him know you have taken care of yourself.

Alerts on strangers in public
You have trained the dog to let you know when the target scents are present. Be prepared to receive an alert in public that may not be to your own BG. Many dogs will actually look toward someone or even attempt to go to them. When this occurs, acknowledge the alert, check yourself and if your BG is normal, move on as possible and cue the dog that you got it. If you get a second alert, recheck yourself to make sure it isn't you.

It is invasive to go up to a stranger and ask if they are a diabetic and tell them your dog says they are low or high. We are not suggesting you walk away from a situation that could be critical, as with someone obviously compromised. The dog will sort this out to a point that they will realize when a situation is critical for your health and when to just be subtle and mention to you that someone is out of range.

Chapter 12

Conclusion

We hope this book has helped you to begin the journey of living and working with a diabetic alert dog. We have found that there are few relationships as rewarding as one forged between a service dog and his devoted, understanding person, and we hope to have set you on the path to becoming such a team. As with all relationships, success depends on realistic expectations, patience, empathy and a commitment to do what it takes to make things work. For the handler of a DAD, this means understanding that the dog is a living being, capable of amazing feats of assistance but also needing ongoing guidance and motivation and the realization that, at the end of the day, he is...a dog. Although a DAD can be a tremendous asset in managing your diabetes, please always remember that you are responsible for your own health.

May you both share long, healthy, happy lives together!

Appendix — Additional Resources by Chapter

Chapter 1: Introduction
Living with a service dog
- *Is a service dog for you?*
  http://herizenfyre-ivil.tripod.com/helperdogs/id3.html

Sources of professionally trained DADs:
- *Finding a reputable DAD program*
  http://www.clickincanines.com/site/choose.html

- *Assistance Dogs International—member programs*
  http://www.assistancedogsinternational.org/membershipd
  irectory.php

- *Owner training vs. professionally/program trained*
  http://www.k9satwork.com/a-otvspro.html

Finding a Trainer:
- *Certification Council for Professional Dog Trainers*
  http://www.ccpdt.org/

- *Karen Pryor Academy*
  http://www.karenpryoracademy.com/find-a-
  trainer?source=kpctnavbar

- *San Francisco SPCA Dog Training Academy trainers list*
  http://www.sfspca.org/resources/library/for-dog-
  owners/dog-trainers-walkers

Chapter 2: Selecting a dog for diabetic alert training

- *Choosing the right dog*
  http://tinyurl.com/alrsr6k

- *Assistance Dogs International (ADI) "Minimum Standards for Assistance Dogs in Public"*
  http://www.assistancedogsinternational.org/Standards/AssistanceDogPublicStandards.php

- *ADI "Public Access Test"*
  http://www.assistancedogsinternational.org/publicaccesstest.php.

- *C-BARQ evaluation*
  http://vetapps.vet.upenn.edu/cbarq/

Chapter 5: Training: Basics and outline
Clicker training

- *Finding a clicker trainer*
  Karen Pryor Academy: Find a great trainer
  http://www.karenpryoracademy.com/find-a-trainer?source=kpctnavbar

- *Clicker training — books*
  The Power of Positive Dog Training (2nd Edition),
  by Pat Miller

  Clicking With Your Dog: Step-By-Step in Pictures,
  by Peggy Tillman

  The Complete Idiot's Guide to Positive Dog Training, 3rd Edition, by Pamela Dennison

Clickertraining – The 4 Secrets of Becoming a Supertrainer,
by Morten Egtvedt & Cecilie Koeste
(eBook available at
http://www.canisclickertraining.com/clickertraining/)

Training Levels – Steps to Success, by Sue Ailsby
(eBook and print books available at
http://www.sue-eh.ca/)

Click for Joy! Questions and Answers from Clicker Trainers and Their Dogs, by Melissa C. Alexander

Don't Shoot the Dog (Revised Edition), by Karen Pryor

- ### Clicker training — DVDs
  The How of Bow Wow – Building, Proofing and Polishing Behaviors,
  by Virginia Broitman & Sherri Lippman

  The Shape of Bow Wow – Shaping Behaviors and Adding Cues, by Virginia Broitman

- ### Clicker training—online videos
  Vancouver Island Assistance Dogs
  http://www.youtube.com/user/supernaturalbc2008

  Emily Larlham (aka KikoPup)
  http://dogmantics.com/free-video-list/

- ### Clicker training — websites
  Clicker Solutions
  http://www.clickersolutions.com/

  Karen Pryor Clicker Training
  http://www.clickertraining.com/

General Guidelines
- ***Recommended reading:*** *Bones Would Rain from the Sky: Deepening our Relationships with Dogs,* by Suzanne Clothier

Chapter 10: Additional skills
Retrieve blood glucose meter, juice box, glucose tablets, etc.
- ***Shirley's Retrieve***
  http://shirleychong.com/keepers/retrieve.html

- ***The Marriage of Target and Retrieve***
  http://www.woofandwordpress.com/targetandretrieve.pdf

Chapter 11: Troubleshooting
- ***Alert and training log sheets***
  http://clickincanines.com/site/pdfs.html

Additional resources
- **Diabetic Alert Dog forum**
  http://diabeticalertdog.com/forum/index.php

Alert Log form

DATE	TIME	BG	ALERT

Sample alert log form. Form can also be found at
http://clickincanines.com/site/pdfs.html

DATE	TIME	BG	ALERT
1/2/2013	8:00 AM	250	YES

Example of how to fill out alert log

Training log form

Simply block in a square for each training session you worked to track what you did for the week. Make notes as you wish.

ALERT	LOW SIGNAL	HIGH SIGNAL	ALERT CHAIN	ALERT CHAIN W SIGNAL	NOTES
WEEKLY TRAINING LOG **Week from** _____ **to** _____					
Color in square per each training session worked through the week					

Sample training log form.

Form can also be found at
http://clickincanines.com/site/pdfs.html

Glossary of terms for
Training Your Diabetic Alert Dog

Note: Definitions given here are specific to use in this book. You may find alternative definitions for these terms in other sources.

Alert: Trained behavior the dog uses to get the attention of the handler when BG is out of range

Alert dog: A dog trained to detect an odor and notify the handler of its presence

Approximations: Steps towards a final behavior

BG: Blood glucose

CGM: Continuous glucose monitor

Chain: A series of behaviors linked together and initiated with a single cue

C/T: Click/Treat; click once and deliver a treat (or other reward) quickly.

Cue: A stimulus (word, physical prompt) that elicits a behavior. For this book, cue is used to mean "verbal cue."

80%+ Rule: Raising the difficulty of a task in training only when the dog is achieving the current level at least 80% of the time (i.e. 4 out of 5, or 8 out of 10 tries). For our purposes, this must be achieved in three training sessions in a row, before raising the difficulty to the next step or level.

Generalization: The process of training the dog to do a behavior (i.e., alert) in any environment, at any time

Pair: Repeating a word with an action (telling the dog what they are doing) to allow the dog to associate the action and word to later become a cue

Pattern: A repeated series of actions

Search dog: A dog trained to precisely locate a target odor (i.e., drugs, explosives) and indicate the location to the handler

Shaping: Building a behavior in small steps, generally by allowing the dog to offer variations of the behavior and reinforcing the ones the trainer likes

Signal: A trained behavior the dog gives to indicate whether a person's BG is low or high

Target: Something the dog is taught to touch with some part of his body (for our purposes, the nose)

"What's up?": Physical and/or verbal action to acknowledge the alert and prompt the signal behavior

About the Authors

Rita Martinez

As a child I was drawn to animals. Many species have moved through my life, but the dog has always been my greatest joy. I have participated in many sports with my dogs, but the gripping nature of scent work is my obsession. I often refer to myself as a scent junkie. I have been training service dogs for over 25 years so the medical alert dog arena is a natural fit for my skills. I feel very fortunate to be able to work in a field that I fully enjoy and that also helps others.

- Over 30 years' experience training dogs in obedience, hunting, search and rescue (tracking, air scent, human remains and water)

- Co-founder of two non-profit organizations involving specialized human remains detection dogs

- Trainer/Owner of Clickin' Canines, LLC. The business works with dog/handler teams incorporating hearing, assistance and medical alert dogs

- Frequent speaker with trainer groups and other service dog organizations wishing to become proficient with the training of diabetic alert dogs for placement

Sue Barns

I discovered the joys of dog training while in graduate school. My first Golden Retriever started me on the journey of learning how dogs and people working as a team can accomplish so much more than either can alone. I explored this partnership in Search and Rescue for several years, a profoundly rewarding experience that set me on the path of service dog training. I am now delighted to find that my experience in various disciplines of dog training, and my skills as a scientist, can be put to use in training assistance dogs and DADs.

- Service dog trainer for Assistance Dogs of the West (Santa Fe, NM), Diabetic Alert Dog program founder

- Over 20 years' experience training dogs for search and rescue (tracking, air scent and human remains), obedience, hunting, therapy, and assistance work. Training Director for obedience, hunting retriever, and search and rescue groups

- Instructor for public dog training classes, search and rescue seminars and assistance dog training classes for students and clients

- Research scientist and assistant professor (Biology; retired)

Acknowledgements

Rita Martinez would like to thank:

Sue Barns, without whom I would not have gotten around to writing a book. In agreeing to share in this project she took on the task of keeping me focused. Because of her training experience and her writing talent, this book is just what I wanted. Sue's ability to keep us moving along with the process has been invaluable. She is truly blessed with patience, as I'd always rather be training dogs than working on a chapter.

My clients and students, for teaching is the true learning experience and they have provided me with an excellent education.

The dogs, as they are my constant instructors. Working with a species without a common language truly levels the playing field. I continue to learn from every dog daily, and have definitely mastered the art of laughing at myself while they join in.

Katerina Lorenzatos Makris, Nancy Weller and Lyn Oppenheim for their encouragement, editing and general support throughout this process.

My husband, **Rupert**, for asking for years why I didn't write a book and when I finally decided to go for it, he didn't complain about all the hours in the office.

Sue Barns would like to thank:

Rita Martinez who, with generosity and grace, freely shared her expertise in DAD training with myself, my colleagues at Assistance Dogs of the West, and many others who sought her help. Her gift has multiplied and changed the lives of our diabetic clients, and I am thankful for the opportunity to help her write this book, that it may offer that gift to many others.

My colleagues and friends at Assistance Dogs of the West who indulged my love of training scent detection dogs by supporting a DAD training program. An amazingly creative and dedicated group, ADW staff, students and volunteers have all contributed time, energy and resources to initiate and sustain the program, in order to provide the unique services of DADs for our diabetic clients.

My clients and their dogs who, of course, have taught me as much as I've taught them, and who continue to inspire me with their dedication, ingenuity, and devotion to each other.

Linda Milanesi, Liz Napieralski and Lynn Wysocki-Smith who lent their editing skills to help make the book as useful, understandable and readable as possible.

Finally, **my amazing husband, Steve,** who supports me in every way, from insightful discussions on all aspects of human (and canine) behavior, to patience for all the things that didn't get done while I was working on this book.